Elephants

by Martin Schwabacher with Lori Mortensen

 **Marshall Cavendish**
Benchmark

New York

Marshall Cavendish Benchmark
99 White Plains Road
Tarrytown, NY 10591
www.marshallcavendish.us

All websites were available and accurate when this book was sent to press.

Library of Congress Cataloging–in–Publication Data

Schwabacher, Martin.
    Elephants / by Martin Schwabacher, with Lori Mortensen.
      p. cm. – (Benchmark rockets. Animals)
    Includes index.
    Summary: "Describes the physical characteristics, habitat, behavior, diet, life cycle, and conservation status of elephants"–Provided by publisher.
    ISBN 978-0-7614-4343-8
 1. Elephants–Juvenile literature. I. Mortensen, Lori, 1955- II. Title.

QL737.P98S397 2010
599.67–dc22
2008052103

Publisher: Michelle Bisson
Editorial Development and Book Design: Trillium Publishing, Inc.

Photo research by Trillium Publishing, Inc.

Cover photo: Shutterstock.com/Robert Hardholt

The photographs and illustrations in this book are used by permission and through the courtesy of:
iStockphoto.com: Chuck Babbit, 1; John Pitcher, 4–5; Lorenzo Pastore, 6; Nico Smit, 12–13; Robert Churchill, 14 (bottom); Steffen Foerster, 15; Peeter Viisimaa, 19; Markus Seidel, 20. Shutterstock.com: Kitch Bain, 8 (top); Andre Maritz, 14 (top). Corbis: Sukree Sukplang/Reuters, 7. Marshall Cavendish Benchmark: 10, 11. Getty Images: Stockbyte, 16–17. Sunny Gagliano: 18. The Elephant Sanctuary in Tennessee: 21.

Printed in Malaysia
1 3 5 6 4 2

Contents

Both male and female African elephants have tusks.

Chapter 1
Living Large

Elephants are the largest land animals in the world. They can grow 10 feet (3 meters) tall and weigh 6 **tons** (5.4 metric tons). Six tons is as heavy as a school bus! Even elephant skin is big. The skin of an elephant weighs one ton all by itself.

Elephants have two giant front teeth called **tusks** that are made of **ivory**. Elephants use their tusks to dig holes and tear bark off of trees. Elephant tusks can grow 7 inches (18 centimeters) a year. The tusks can get as long as 11 feet (3.4 m).

Elephants have a special nose called a **trunk**. A trunk is kind of like a nose,

5

This elephant uses its trunk to reach leaves high up in the tree.

arm, hand, and water hose all in one. Elephants pinch together the fingerlike tips of their trunks to pick up things. They use their trunks to suck up water just like a straw. Then they spray water into their mouths with their trunks. Elephants also use their trunks to make sounds. Sometimes an elephant's trunk makes a sound like a trumpet.

Elephants are big eaters. They can eat up to 300 pounds (136 kilograms) of food in a day. They eat grass, fruit, leaves, bark, and branches. In fact, a hungry elephant will eat a whole tree, from the roots to the leaves! Elephants spend 16 hours a day eating. Often they have to walk about 40 miles (64 kilometers) a day looking for food and water. They travel between 3,000 and 6,000 miles (4,800 to 9,700 km) a year.

An elephant's **brain** is bigger than the brain of any other land animal. Having a big brain helps an elephant do clever things. An elephant can use tools, unlike most animals. If an elephant has an itch, it might use a stick to scratch the itch. Elephants have been known to throw trees at electric fences that were meant to keep them out of a farmer's field. Some elephants have figured out how to open doors and locks.

Some elephants in Thailand have been taught to paint. They hold the paintbrush with the tip of their trunks.

Young elephants often hold their mother's tail while they walk. This is like a child holding its mother's hand.

Baby elephants have a lot to learn. One important thing they need to learn is how to use their trunks. At first, their trunks wiggle out of control. Sometimes baby elephants trip over their trunks. They suck on their trunks, too, just like a human baby sucks on its thumb.

Elephants have good memories. An elephant can remember where a **waterhole** is, even if it has been years since it was last there.

Once a day, elephants drink at a waterhole. They drink up to 50 gallons (190 liters) of water at a time. That's enough to fill a bathtub! Elephants like salt, too. Elephants find salt by digging holes in the ground with their tusks.

Elephants are born big. They are 3 feet (1 m) tall and weigh about 250 pounds (113 kg) when they are born. A baby elephant weighs as much as a large man! A baby elephant grows inside its mother for almost two years. That's more than twice as long as a human baby grows inside its mother.

Baby elephants drink milk for up to four years. Every day, the baby gets bigger and bigger. By the time it is five years old, the baby will weigh over 1,000 pounds (450 kg). The elephant will keep growing. Unlike other animals, an elephant grows all its life.

There are two kinds of elephants–African and Asian. African elephants are bigger than Asian elephants. African elephants have bigger ears and more wrinkles on their skin than Asian elephants do. The trunks of African and Asian

Comparing African and Asian Elephants

African Elephant

- bigger
- larger ears
- more wrinkles
- two "fingers" on trunk
- no hump on forehead
- both males and females have tusks

elephants are different, too. An African elephant has two "fingers" at the end of its trunk. An Asian elephant only has one "finger." Asian elephants have a hump on their forehead, but African elephants do not. Only male Asian elephants have tusks, but both male and female African elephants have tusks.

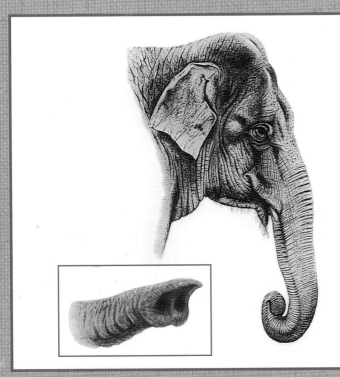

Asian Elephant

- smaller
- smaller ears
- fewer wrinkles
- one "finger" on trunk
- hump on forehead
- only males have tusks

This elephant family is drinking at Samburu National Reserve in Kenya. Can you tell what kind of elephants they are?

Chapter 2
Elephant Families

Elephants live in **herds**. Each herd is a family made up of female elephants and their young. There may be up to 20 females in a herd. The oldest female is the leader. She knows how to find food and water. She knows how to keep the herd safe.

Males do not live with the herd. They live alone or with other males. Male elephants visit herds to mate and to protect their young. Male elephants fight each other over females during mating time. The strongest males get to mate. This makes the herd stronger.

Elephants can live in different habitats.

Elephants have learned to live in many **habitats**. Some elephants live in forests and grasslands. Some live in marshes and mountains. Some elephants even live in deserts! Desert elephants eat grass when it rains. In the dry season, they eat leaves from thorny trees and bushes. Desert elephants have to travel farther to find water than other elephants do. If the herd does not find water, its members will die.

Elephants like to be around each other. They rub against each other. They touch each other with their trunks. Sometimes they put their trunks in each other's mouths!

Elephants talk to each other using many different sounds. They purr, grunt, and growl. They blast, rumble, and squeal. Some elephant sounds are so low that people cannot hear them—but elephants can. These low sounds travel for miles. People believe elephants use the low sounds to talk to herds that are far away.

Elephants take care of each other's babies. They care for other elephants when they are sick. Elephants will risk their lives to protect their family. When an elephant is about to die, its family gathers around. After it is dead, the herd cries. The herd may guard the body for hours. Sometimes they cover the body with brush. Many people believe elephants visit the bones of their dead family members.

These two elephants are using their trunks to say hello to each other.

15

Hunters have killed thousands of elephants for their ivory tusks.

Chapter 3
The Last Giants

Elephants live for 45 to 60 years. They are so big that other animals are usually not a problem for them. But something else can be a big problem— their teeth! Elephants cannot stop their teeth from wearing out. Elephants get six sets of teeth during their life. When one set wears out, another set takes its place. Elephants need their teeth to grind leaves and branches. When their last set of teeth wears out, elephants cannot chew. Without food, they die.

The biggest danger to elephants is not worn-out teeth. It's people. One hundred years ago, there were 5 to 10 million elephants in Africa. Today there are fewer than one million.

There were 100,000 elephants in Asia one hundred years ago. Today there are fewer than 35,000. As people moved into elephant country and turned the land into farmland, there was less land for elephants. Elephants did not have enough to eat and many elephants died.

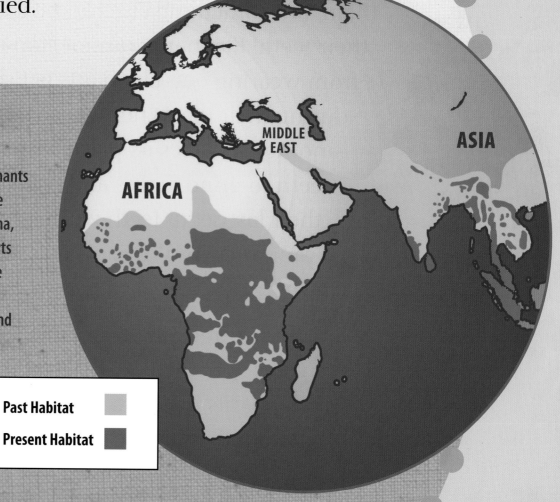

This map shows where elephants used to live and where they live now. Elephants have disappeared from the Middle East, Pakistan, China, Java, South Africa, and parts of eastern Africa. There are some elephants still living in India, Southeast Asia, and western Africa.

Past Habitat

Present Habitat

Hunters have also killed millions of elephants to get their tusks. Elephant tusks are made of ivory, which is very beautiful. Hunters sold the tusks to people who then used the ivory to make things like combs and jewelry. People made laws to try to stop the hunting of elephants. These laws didn't work. Hunters made too much money selling tusks. A single tusk was worth thousands of dollars. So hunters kept on killing elephants.

Many elephants have lost their lives so that ivory carvings such as this one could be made.

People made a new law to protect elephants. The law said people could not sell things made out of ivory. The price of ivory went down when people could not sell ivory things. Hunters could no longer make money by selling tusks, and most hunters stopped killing elephants.

Today, people are working together to protect elephants. People are learning that they don't have to turn elephant land into farmland. They can make money from people coming to see the elephants. Many countries have created national parks. These parks save land for elephants and other wild animals.

These elephants live in Tsavo National Park in Kenya. The park protects elephants and other wild animals.

Even with the parks, elephants are still in danger. As time goes on, people and elephants will continue to face problems. People will need to continue to save land for elephants and make strong laws to protect them. It is the only way to save these gentle giants.

Shirley (left) and Bunny (right) both came to live at The Elephant Sanctuary in 1999. Shirley had been in the circus and Bunny had spent her life in a zoo. Both of these elephants are about 60 years old.

People are saving elephants in other places, too. Elephants that used to live in circuses and zoos are finding new homes. One home is The Elephant Sanctuary in Hohenwald, Tennessee. It's the largest elephant preserve in the United States.

Glossary

brain: The part of the body found in the skull. It is the mind and control center of the body.

habitats: Places where plants or animals grow or live in nature.

herds: Groups of elephants or other animals that live together.

ivory: The smooth, hard material that tusks are made of.

tons: Units of weight. One ton is two thousand pounds.

trunk: The long, powerful nose of an elephant.

tusks: The two long teeth on each side of an elephant's mouth.

waterhole: A small pond or pool that has water in it.

Find Out More

Books

Bloom, Steve, and David Henry Wilson. *Elephants: A Book for Children*. New York: Thames and Hudson, 2008.

Buckley, Carol. *Just for Elephants*. Gardiner, ME: Tilbury House Publishers, 2006.

Joubert, Dereck. *Face to Face with Elephants*. Des Moines, IA: National Geographic Children's Books, 2008.

Schlaepfer, Gloria. *Elephants* (AnimalWays). New York: Marshall Cavendish, 2003.

Schwabacher, Martin. *Elephants* (Animals Animals). New York: Marshall Cavendish, 2001.

Stewart, Melissa. *Elephants*. New York: Children's Press, 2002.

Websites

National Geographic Kids
http://kids.nationalgeographic.com/Animals/CreatureFeature/African-elephant/

PBS (from the television show *Nature*)
http://www.pbs.org/wnet/nature/elephants

The Elephant Sanctuary
http://www.elephants.com/sanct.htm

Index

Page numbers for photographs and illustrations are in **boldface**.